77 Sonnets and Thirty-Six SONGS

Tom Basham

A SunJen Publication

SunJen Publications is a subsidiary of SAP Films

www.tombasham.com

ISBN 10: 0-9968548-3-5
ISBN 13: 978-0-9968548-3-2

Cover Design by Custom Designers, Inc., Nokesville, Virginia
Interior Formatting by Victor Rook

Contents

Thirty-Six Songs

Foreword

Poets tell the truth. We have to. When "post-modernism" evolves into "post-truth" and some 60 million of us seem content with the concept of "alternative facts," someone has to be honest. Leave it to the poets. When I think of the places where dishonest, snake-oil salespeople slather me with their particular brand of bullshit – the nightly news, the editorial section of the paper, any of the 1,978 channels broadcasting 24 hours a day, Facebook, Twitter, the classroom, the college lecture hall, even the cereal aisle – I reach for my favorite collections and take comfort in knowing that poets remain truth tellers. Such is the case with Tom Basham's "77 Sonnets and 36 Songs." Tom's honest. He's been writing poetry for longer than many of us have been alive, and his debut collection draws from decades of sonnets, pure rhyme, song lyrics, and napkin scribbles he's collected since inheriting his Uncle Bill's typewriter in the 1970s. Tom holds nothing back in "77 Sonnets and 36 Songs," permitting us to read over his shoulder while he mines deeply into his life, loves, disappointments, celebrations, and tragedies. From a helium balloon fading into clouds to a glass of Scotch as a record of his highs and lows, Tom paints images and deals metaphors like playing cards in this ample collection of nearly 50 years of poetry and song. But don't expect rose colored glasses. Tom's mileage – some of it clearly down dirt roads – shows in his stark, to-the-point, no-bullshit style. His muse is a "bitch," an honest one. Thankfully, he grants us some time with her in his debut collection.

Robert Scott, Poet and author of the Sailor Doyle mysteries

Dedication

This collection of contextualized communication is dedicated to my Uncle Bill, "Hillard Amburgey" (1933-1974). He was one of my Mom's brothers, her favorite I think, and he lived with us for a while when I was a kid. He was a giant man – probably 6' 5" or better and the quiet type, spending most of his time with coffee and cigarettes. He was a gentle soul who had seen things in the war and had quite the hand tremor to show for it.

What I remember most about him was that he wrote poetry. He would sit at the dining room table and type on an old Smith Corona manual typewriter. I had been writing poetry for years before he showed up, but not at the kitchen table. I was not so bold, nor was I brave enough to connect with him as a writer. A few years after he left our home he moved to Alaska and died.

I don't know how I came by it (thanks Mom,) but I got custody of his typewriter and his corduroy sport coat (46 long). Both went to college with me in 1977 and I typed many a poem and school paper on that typewriter. I would put on that sport coat that enveloped me and consumed by the restless spirit of a fellow word wrangler, I roamed the streets of Blacksburg, Va., and the Virginia Tech campus. I still have the typewriter and that sport coat is in horrible condition, but I can't let it go. I did not know my Uncle Bill well – or really much at all. I just know that to look at him, the last thing you would think of him was that he was a poet. I think most people would say the same thing about me – and I'm okay with that.

To my Uncle Bill, whose two-finger typing of his poems at my Mom's dining room table inspires me every day.

Uncle Bill and Mom

Introduction

I have been writing poetry for five decades and most of it has never been read or heard by another human being. I have shared a bit with a few and the usual response is one of a parent when their kid gets a "C" on his report card. I try not to take this as an actual critique. I think it's a cross between they don't understand and don't know what to say. This book represents my first major effort to get some of this out there – 'cause I had to get it out of me. I'll be fine if this merely allows me to collect more dumbfounded looks.

I have never been hung on perfect form and meter – that's not what poetry is about. I always considered anything with 14 lines a sonnet, and since my High School English Teacher bestowed upon me *"Poetic License,"* I am therefore justified. When I read that Shakespeare published 154 sonnets, I first said "Wow!," and then counted how many I had. There was a bunch, and I decided these 77 were ready to go. That's half Shakespeare and that's not half bad…and unlike him, I'm not dead yet.

Just about all the verse I write rhymes. I don't know why – it's probably a sickness – like "Rhymin Simon" disease. I have never written for profit, but I realized that the highest paid writers out there are poets. People like John Lennon, Paul Simon, James Taylor… Springsteen. We don't think of them as poets, but they are. So, as I started assembling this collection I started to wonder if any of my sonnets could be songs.

Sonnet: Derived from the Italian word "sonetto". A small or little song or lyric.

I went through my sonnets and decided that I just couldn't take this bundle of words and sew together a song. So I started all over and decided to abandon poetry and write songs. I know this sounds like giving up beer for ale, but that conscious decision made all the difference. Knowing that I was writing a song and not a poem put melodies in my head along with the vision of Jackson Browne belting it out on stage.

The logic with 77 sonnets, as explained above, is sound, and it would seem that having 36 songs was a mere continuation of alliteration. At first I wanted to do twelve songs, one album – remember albums? When the songs kept coming, I realized that anybody can write a good song, or even have a good album but if someone has three great albums they will be immortal. Therefore, the number is just an attempt at immortality. Don't try to ready anything more into it.

I don't know if any of this is any good, but I know I had to do it, write it, express it, own it and ultimately have the guts to let you people see it.

"It's only words, and words are all I have to take your heart away"

Barry, Robin & Maurice Gibb

The Soul Of A Poet

The soul of a poet - I don't know what that is,

How it can breathe, or where it might live.

How it may evolve, exist or emote,

Or how it lays claim to the verses I wrote.

These things don't appear to me out of thin air,

They're not manufactured with computer hardware.

They come when I suffer, confront and confide,

In the demons I battle that tend to reside,

Inside of my heart, and outside of my head,

Or muttered into something I wished I had said

Out loud to the world, so maybe they'd see

There was something they didn't know about me

And the soul of a poet that can only be found

In the words of the verse I choose to write down.

Joy

You can look upon the surface or deeper if you dare
To look inside the words, you'll find you're everywhere

My life is in my verse, as these decades unfold
Besides unbridled pain is the promise that you hold

When I speak of love, you've taught and I have learned
And when I write of loss, it's for you I have yearned

Don't try and figure how, or even when it seems
These words came to be or what is in the dream

Each verse explores a feeling and how it felt for me
And while I recall the reeling, I have no memory

Of the source of the emotion, a fountain lost in time
A spout to ink my thoughts into words that tend to rhyme

I know this in my heart, and I hope you know it too,
Every poem I have written is eventually about you

This I Believe

This I believe,

and this is what I've found,

The stories in my mind,

must be written down.

They tell of dreams

and simple things

That touch us in our souls -

At times they bring

a heart to sing.

Or laugh or lose control.

For I believe I must conceive

The essence of a man,

To get it said, to have it read,

I'll do the best I can.

My Muse is a Bitch

My muse gets on my nerves, that's just part of her plan

She has to make these swerves you would never understand

She gets under my skin and demands I give her time

Demands I let her in and demands that I opine

On visions of the day, and dreams I can't control

And what my mind would say, if I was ten years old

And I didn't know the world had a plan for me,

A place, a job, a girl, and not a fantasy

But she won't let me 'lone, the unrequited bitch,

Each day I must atone and make the choice of which

Horizon I will drive to, awake or in a dream

My heart demands I strive to serve the one that seems

Like coffee in my cup to help me face the day

So when my time is up, I had something to say

Blue Shoes

Blue shoes on the dryer, size 3 or maybe size 4,
Crayon colored artwork, cover the 'frigerator door.

The signs are there, a glance and it seems clear,
There are some little people living around here.

Blue shoes on the dryer, the laces tied in a knot,
Little feet had slipped them off and soon they were forgot.

Until a mother's hand, scooped them from the floor,
And placed them on the dryer...size 3 or maybe size 4.

Blue shoes on the dryer, school menu by the phone,
I only see one mitten, the other did not come home.

I don't know the footsteps, the troubles of these shoes,
The cans they have kicked, the puddles they stomped through

Every day is new, they are put to the test,
The blue shoes on the dryer, for a moment are at rest...

NO-Stalgia

I know why we love nostalgia, I finally figured it out
It's not that we cling to the past like that's what we're all about
  Things we recall are a comfort – that old movie is our friend
With that song we remember things were better than we pretend
  We love something that's familiar, so our past is a great place to go
We really don't like surprises – we only like what we know
  Because if there is something new or something we've never seen
How will we know if we like it – how will we know what it means
  Cause I don't know what will happen If I let something else in
And it's not like I've always known and it's not somewhere I've been
  How will I be comfortable if this is something new
What makes you think this will be something I want to do
  I can't let go of the past like the blanket when you're a kid
Who knows what you could do if you let go of what you did

Climbing Out Of Sleep

Climbing out of sleep, after climbing out of bed

Am I in the day – or in the dream instead?

Gathering my thoughts, lathering in the dawn

I can barely focus, or muster up a yawn

Taking every step, making my way

It's all muscle memory, my worries are at bay

I am at a loss, the dream has made a call

I think I could go back, and have her after all

I resort to the James Taylor, the Beatles were all wrong

A day in the life, was much more than a song

I see it all now, so I know it must be so

My life has a purpose, and for that I have to go

Climb out of my sleep, and into the world,

Right into the arms, of my baby girl.

Under the Radar

Under the radar, into the port –
Not to be seen, or be out of sorts
Never to know the feelings inside
The depth of the soul, the surge of the tide
Never to see wherever you go
Always alone, never to know
The hand of another causing a sigh
Claiming the path of wandering eyes
Into the night and into the dawn
Believe that tomorrow may not be gone
Lost in the wind, destined to find
Another horizon, another time
When there is a breeze pointed at you
Under the radar, just out of view

The Balloon

You know I had that empty feeling - I was lost in the afternoon
Like I dropped my ice-cream cone... I let go of my balloon

I watched it fade away, 'til it became the clouds,
And I became alone, like the faces in the crowd

And I almost reached out, for the sake of my dismay
But I had not star to stand on, I did not know the way

Yet I had that damn balloon, should I have held it tight?
Should I confine it to my hand? Do I have that right?

Did it want to go away - or was it just the sky?
Did I really let it go? Who knows the reason why?

It just kept on climbing, in lieu of my contest,
I had a special feeling, it had a special quest.

I should have called upon a tear, but my feelings tend to hide,
I just watched it float away, with an empty feeling inside...

Hi

Hi
Sigh
I
Shy
Try
Vie
Tie
Lie
Cry
Sigh
Why
My
Tie
Die

The Drawer

You're reaching for my love, I'm reaching out for you

Who lives in ever after, who shares the things we do

You call upon my conscious, a call I can't abide

I'm landing in your heart, you're landing by my side

I wish I could explain, it's something I can't do

If you can't be in my arms, I won't be holding you

And I won't be holding on, but I'd like to let you know

Leave me in your heart, if you're next to letting go

I'll put you in a drawer, but I'll keep you on top

Like something that I've started, and something I can't stop

It's not a real bad place, there's nothing to discard

I only know discretion and loneliness are hard

Perhaps I'll pull you out someday, and treat you like I could

Or climb inside there with you, or let you think I would

Could Have Been

I always had a dream for you

I had the faith and vision to

See beyond the world concerns

I held the dream, you tossed and turned

You saw the storm, I saw the same

You fled the shore – it was only rain

We fit together like a puzzle locks

But you never saw the picture on the box

It's hard to know what to trust

When all you paint will turn to rust

I always had a dream for you

You lived your life and never knew

That upon me you could depend

You had no faith in could have been

How Many Words

How many words – how many lines
How many pages – how many times
Do I have to write everything down
Does every emotion have to be found
Captured in characters, syllables and such
Can the feelings I feel matter that much
That they be recorded for someone to read
To know what I say, and what I need
To be understood and to understand
Before I may lose the voice in my hand
I need to acknowledge, accept and agree
It's something that's always been inside of me
The verse and the volumes of stories I tell
Are left so that others may know me well

Maybe We're Connected

Maybe we're connected, somewhere across the plane,
Maybe we're connected, or maybe we're the same.

Drawn to have these visions, where life's not what it seems,
Descending into darkness, embracing one last dream.

Maybe we're connected, two parts that make a whole,
We can never function, without each other's soul

If I could hold forever, in the middle of my hand,
And cultivate the future, as if I owned the land

Then I could start believing, in the soul of now and then
Of maybes and tomorrows, and what's around the bend.

If I could hold a moment, in the midst of passing time,
Of day to day horizons, the rhythms and the rhymes

Then if I could have forever, in the cradle of my hand
And I could see tomorrow, and begin to understand

How Do I

How do I love thee, let me count the ways
How do I care for thee, let me start today.
How long shall I be with thee, just long enough to say
How much that I think of thee, for how much I display
How do I sing for thee, how shall I write this song
How shall I play for thee, how shall I belong
How long shall I plead with thee, for thee to be along
How long shall I be with thee, before I see it's wrong
How do I wish for thee, in never ending dream,
How long shall I think of thee, or how long shall it seem
How shall I call out for thee, when I cannot see,
How shall all my time with thee, be my memories
How shall I pray for thee, how shall cast my prayers
How shall I be leaving thee, how shall I hold my tears.

Just a Thing

It's just a day, it's just a thing
  There's no reason to bring
    Yesterday's attitude
From last week's interlude
  That took you off your game
    And you still wear the blame
      Of walking in unprepared
Believing they would not have cared
  Who you were and what you thought
    What you said and what you brought
      So suck it up and get a clue
This is what you're meant to do
  Take a breath and think again
    Why you're here and where you've been

Builder's Sonnet

What's a boy to build, when he's come to understand,
The labor of his love, has made a broken man
   The visions of his youth now tower in the sky,
They became foundations within the reasons why
   Forsaken by a plan, and captured by the stage
The instrument of artists, humbled by the page
   For him it's a religion, for others just a trade,
The earth would lay in wait, the sculpting of his spade
   He would hold a sermon, in the light of afternoon,
And pay homage to the shadow he had caused to loom
   Yet in the waning sunset, a truth came to be known,
There's more than bricks and mortar, in the building of a home
   And in the days to come, his future will be found
For what's a boy to build, when his dreams have been torn down

Thoughts

I've lost my train of thought, I had it a second ago
I was somewhere doing something and somehow I ought to know
If I could have a minute and a little quiet too
I'm sure I could remember what I was going to do
I may seem distracted and my focus lingers away
And I'm on to the next thing and that might be okay
But I was on a mission – felt like it was do or die
And I know it was important – I just can't remember why
I'm not going crazy – I don't think I'm going there
That might be my destination in a couple more years
Right now I think I'm tired – my body tells me that
My mind is a little moody like a tire that has a flat
So don't expect too much and I won't let you down
I think I am here with you but my thoughts are out of town

Distant Dreams

Distant dreams forever seem, destined to our past

Candles lit to see the glow continue to contrast

Like the poet's endless love, imprisoned by his pen

Forever is a daydream ever to pretend

Days bring years, beyond the time our futures will unfold

Let time become the reason for the reason to be told

For if the night befell the moon and life a feathered nest

The dawn would bring the sunshine, a journey, and a quest

Through fields all but hidden in the forest of our mind

The light between the seasons let the reasons be unkind

Off beyond the laughter, the candle casts a glow

Foreseen is ever after, for all that we shall know

That light shall never darken, though dim it yields despair

Perhaps it shall be destined to be forever there

Is It Real

What is this – is it real?

Or maybe to make me feel

Closer to a point of view

Less inclined to think of you

In the ways I have heard

What they say must be absurd

Yet maybe truth is not a riddle

And I'm not stuck here in the middle

Listening and choosing sides

Sentiment shifts with the tide

Tangents running everywhere

And I wonder why you care

If I keep an open mind

And the truth will be revealed in time

Why Do I Hurt Thee…

I hurt you cause you hold, what I do not possess,
Or maybe what I need, or desire to caress.

I hurt you cause I'm scared, or I don't live like you,
Or maybe I just hurt you, cause my leaders tell me to

I hurt you to protect, what's behind my walls,
Or maybe cause somebody, hurt me when I was small

I hurt you cause I wanted, to be part of the show,
Or maybe I have hurt you, so everyone will know -

That I'm the one that hurt you, because I hurt inside,
Maybe I just hurt you, and there is no reason why

I may start with words, to try and bend your will,
But if that doesn't work, I'll turn to fists and steel

Take away the weapons, and be prepared to see,
I will inflict pain, cause it's inside me.

Throughout the Rain

Throughout the rain a wind prevails
Across the sea, upon my sails
I cast my darkness through the day
Relinquishing the words I say
I fall for you with open arms
I come to mean you no harm
For I have reached for love and touch

And found with you life ain't that much

I call for you in my dismay
I'm mesmerized by your display
I reach with words to hold a dream
And have a love for what it seems
Yet never touch and just be there
Reach with your heart, if you intend to care

The Voyage

Cast land aside and climb aboard, we see the setting sun
Haul that line and set the course, beneath new horizons
Hoist the main, set the jib, the winds are light today
The sea is smooth and friendly - steer by the rudder's sway
We'll surely make the island, it's practically in sight
The breeze now from the east, has the canvas drawn and tight
For so long a destination, a vision of trees and rock
And now it's just a place to tie up at the dock
The night falls with a flash, from the starboard side view
And the rainbow does a dance, with the rhythm of the blues
There's no chocolate on pillows, or beds found tucked in well
We sleep in the berth of travelers, a song the lanyards tell
For the sea will call tomorrow, and you can't put her on hold
The voyage must be taken, and the story must be told

Reaching

You reach for me, you don't let go
You do not see that I don't know
You think I care because I call
You think it matters if I see you fall
You think I'll be there, and I just might
You think tomorrow, and I think tonight
You claim the hour begs the time
You let the past become a crime
You are almost always right,
I'm almost always there each night
From the start and quite far along
From the beginning, it's more right than wrong
To give it a chance, to see it through
If you reach from me, and I reach for you

Writer's Class Sonnet
Circa '84

I'm really not a writer, I just write things down,
I really just dropped by ..... for your verbs and your nouns.
    I used to be creative, but not anymore,
I used to have a passion but lately I'm not sure.

    Most of you are published, your words have worth and praise,
I come to share your wisdom, you see I've lost my way.
    You're all so deep in talent, in poetry and prose,
Each time a work of art becomes what you compose.

    Just don't ask me to read, it's not that I am scared,
You see I'm really not a writer, and besides I'm not prepared.
    So pleased move right along, I can't be more sincere,
I'm searching for the key, while imprisoned in my fear.
    For now I'll sit and listen, I hope you understand....
Though I'm really not a writer, I hope one day I am.

Scotch Story

If scotch could tell a story, without telling a lie
Then I'm thirsty for a memory, so pour a couple lines
The truth is at the door, I can hear it knock
It's been a while since it opened, I'll take it on the rocks
Beyond the decisions that set me on this road
I thought I'd turned a corner and lightened up my load
Time can heal a wound, but it tends to leave a scar
Like the dark and cloudy night hides away the stars
Some moments have been captured in the family photo book
I'd forgotten all the good times and the pictures that we took
All the smiles at Christmas, Birthdays and Easter too
The old cars we have had and the children as they grew
It's easy in a picture to miss take up for down
So pour another story, and I'll write another round

A Vision of You

There is a vision – just in view,
I take my pen and think of you
Tortured souls with broken hearts
Who know the suffering pain imparts.
I create words like twisted steel,
To describe my life and how I feel
Alone in darkness, shadows blend,
Upon the light I must depend
Until a vision struck my eyes
And as it formed I realized
This may not be a dream
And I might find out what it means
All the nights I thought of you
Before we came into view

I Never Said I Love You

I never said I love you - never spoke the words.
I never let my feelings be verbally conferred.

    I spoke behind my eyes,
Though my arms may hold a clue,
      Of maybe where my heart was,
As I held it close to you

    At times I may have mumbled,
And hinted at a dream
      My voice may have been silent,
But inside my head it screamed

    Do not promise tomorrow
Cause it may never be
      So I never said I love you,
But you never said you loved me.

Verbal Crutches

To be honest, is the worst pre-amble,
To tell the truth would be another gamble.
Just say what you will, if it is your place -
The fact of the matter will not make your case.

I'd just like to say, never needs to be said,
And nobody ever wanted to be caught dead.
I know I'm not alone when I use a verbal crutch,
Cause at the end of the day does not mean that much

Though I appreciate the thought in the interest of time,
Don't beat around the bush with the bottom line,
Cause I know what it'll be, when it is like this -
When you have the last word I don't want to miss.
Let me be clear, you may have jumped the gun,
I'm sorry, but this will not get the job done.

Change of Seasons

I love the change of seasons, they alter night and day,
As much as rhymes and reasons reveal what I can't say

I'm caught up in believing that time imprisons pain,
For life can be deceiving, like rainbows and the rain

Cause all I do is think of you, your wisdom and your grace,
Although I've gone a far and few, you've given me a place

You offer such a candid style, infused with your intent,
I long each day to make you smile – I drown in pure content

I've always been at home with you, as if I'd had a dream,
I lie in bed at half past two, amazed at what I've seen

You make the autumn colors warm, you are the last sunset,
You are my quilt for winter storms, you are beautiful and yet

You are my own horizon, and you are unaware,
You are my change of seasons, you are my here to there.

Blinds

I see the world through venetian blinds

Segmented into horizontal lines

Broken down into tiny sections

Slices of life for my inspection.

The curtain back, the sun comes in

The shadows crawl, long and thin

Here is the life that I can afford

Apportioned by the plain white cord.

I know there is more in the world for me

I won't be satisfied by what I see

Twenty-seven pictures of snow as it falls

If I had the courage I would raise it all

And piece together something brand new

Or just go outside and embrace the view.

Human Beings

How to be

You and me

What is so

Apropos

Maybe not

I forgot

What I can

Understand

And be seeing

Human beings

With a knack

To interact

And become

With someone

Falling into Love

They say you fall into love
Lose your balance, like you're shoved
Into a thing you can't escape
You can't avoid or navigate
Around the buoys, starboard side
Just like the moon controls the tide
It's not a choice you can allude
Involuntary servitude
You put your heart into their hands
You put your thoughts at their command
By the time it happens, it's too late
They may not even reciprocate
But if they do, you can't go wrong
Until that day when it's all gone

Hamster Wheel

I'd like to get off the hamster wheel
Been on this thing my whole life and still
I can't get to the destination
I know I was just improving my station
Try as I might I just can't get there
And I was thinking about going elsewhere
To a place where they don't worship money
Before I go to the land of milk and honey
I'd like to find out what I have learned
And less about what I have earned
And more about what it all means
The life and death and the stuff in between
And maybe I could do what I may,
But I'll have to go to work today

Whispered Bye

A whispered bye
A half-turned eye
A smile kept inside
No adieu to abide
That hint of a sound
That head turned down
Wanting to play
With her friend today
Gramps please sit down
To ease the frown
We can stack blocks
Or play knock knock
Or say goodbye
And hear the cry

Appearances

Why might I leave this day
And wander from your field
You cannot care for what I say
For what I come to yield
Yet I care for what you are
And how you think of me
Blind can even see the stars
Easier than we
Be the past passed today
Tomorrow's not so near
Listen not to what I say
And not how I appear
Know we'll always have
The dream of yester-year

Passive Aggressive God

We have a passive aggressive God, he won't come when you call
Pick you up when you fall, but he's in every cell of your bod.

You think you love God the most, you speak to him on Sunday
Forget him on Monday, and cite the bible in Facebook posts

You may call it intelligent design, because there is a creator,
He's not the narrator, you must choose to believe without signs

Faith is belief without knowing, you can stay off your knees,
Blame him for disease, and not really know where you're going

It's not all about fear and sin, you can read the good book,
And still not be shook, to believe he will come back again

Maybe God has nothing to say, cause it's all up to you,
And your primordial ooze, to decide what you're gonna do

Take the big bang that science okay'd, cause God lit the fuze
So please don't abuse, the magic my God has made

Obligated

It was hanging there this morning, it stalked me all night long.
There is no getting past it, and I did nothing wrong.
I have got to do this, I know that I should,
I wish I'd just stay quiet, and not said that I would,
Cause now I'm obligated, no choice, it must be done,
It's not like there's a contract, or it's something for my mum,
I guess I could speak up, I could just say no,
They would never forget it, and they'd never let it go,
I'd always have the guilt, for what I didn't do,
Because I turned my back, when they asked me to.
It's just become expected, for me to deal with this
Everyone will watch me, and everyone will miss,
The anger that I bury – I'll keep that to my self,
Next time when this needs doing, I'll be somewhere else.

I've Come To Be Alone

I've come to be alone, in the kingdom of my friend
I've come to find a solitude in the beginning and the end
I'd like to take the noise as rustling in the wind,
The pain preserves a version my vision can't condemn
At times I think they're shallow, and short on what it takes
At times I'm sure they've lost it when they try to compensate
They're not quite what I am, the side they will never see
They're don't know who I am, or who that I will be
So why must I compete against my fellow man
It's really not my place to make them understand
There is no need for anger, so leave it on the shelf
And take away the solace you promised for yourself
Just rest alone in silence, you can't argue with the dawn
You can only feed the pain with the dreams you come upon

Am I With You

Hello my friend
Am I with you
Or am I here
Just passing through
If I am here
Will you be there
Or does it matter if I care
I have seen
Those eyes before
For I can't see you anymore
Do you live to be
With me
Or have I lost
What we could be

Benefit of the Doubt

I rarely benefit from the doubt
That's really not what trust is about
There may be reasons to believe
There may be facts meant to deceive
What you think that I would do
What they said and what I told you
And every morning you think – no
By the end of the day - it's I don't know
You want to trust and believe in me
But like the rest, you wait and see
It becomes less about the facts
And more about the way you act
When that doubt comes creeping in
And if you will ever trust again.

I am – Not

I made a picture, when I cannot draw
I wrote a song, when I can't sing at all
I can make a movie no one will see
I can hold the vision of what I want to be
I can build a house but I can't make a home
I'm okay in a group, but I prefer being alone
I really work hard, I'm successful but instead
Of having lots of money I can't seem to get ahead
I know lots of people, and they think they know me
This is probably normal, the way that it should be
I'd really like to travel, but I don't' want to go anywhere
I help a lot of people, but I'm not sure they care
I'm quick to tell a joke, or get off a funny line
I know I should be happy, but I'm not most of the time

Another Sunny Day

Another sunny day I've spent
The hours pass without relent
And when my time of work is through
I settle down to think of you
I think you're it, but I wonder why
In my life I'd pass you by
Allowing thoughts of wishful things
And wait for what the future brings
But if the future's like the past
And if it seems that we could last
When all our times together tolled
Something we have never known
For when I talk to you again
Our time will have come to an end

Maybe Once a Year

Maybe once a year, you reach into your soul,
And find what keeps you sane, and barely in control.
   You hold it in your hand, and then take it for a ride,
It's time to lose control, so you toss it over the side
   Across the new horizon, just beyond the sun
The light from yesterday we never thought would come
   There's a power in the moonlight, beyond the twilight twinge
It may have only surfaced, but it always lay within
   And then you're on your own, and you find you're not the
same,
There are no more obligations, and no one else to blame.
   I call today tomorrow, but it's just the day before
I call the past the sorrow, I'm lost in the either or
   And life showed me a meaning, in the never ending pain,
For the truth becomes tomorrow, and the sorrow tends to wane

Look at ME

Look at me
This is me
I am right over here
Have you met me
You would like me
I can't be more sincere

Listen to me
It's about me
I am someone you should know
I can't sing
Or anything
Just give me time to show,

I am more than I seem to be,
And you should have noticed me.

Destiny

Destiny's a bitch, and a player at the same time,

Inside you she will guide you along the proper lines

The path is not straight, so look out for the turns

You'll wander and ponder and become quite concerned

Don't look in the darkness to maybe find the light

In the smallest of all of us lies the most fight

To search for the meaning and how it is made

When essentially, eventually you ride the last cascade

If you wade through the sorrow of supposed to be's

You'll get wet and forget to look out and see

Our journey has delivered us to this place

More enlightened than frightened, and just in case

All our tomorrows will come out just right

Our dreams may redeem their purpose and sight

Loneliness

Loneliness… like never ending sorrow,
　Searching for the day, that may precede tomorrow
Thoughts of one upon my past, maybe one I knew
　Or maybe only memories of the dreams you once slept through

Wasted times of solitude, you thought you were alone,
　Let what you see not deceive, before it can be shown
Could all my days, upon my past, return to me now?
　We may re-live our shattered time, shall we learn somehow

Might I've known about the truth, would I have told a lie?
　Or would I let a costly thing, such as this pass by?
　　Redeem the time we almost had, yet keep it in the mind,
　　　Let the heart beseech the soul, for it can be defined –
　　　　And only live to re-believe what I can't regret…
The years to come won't let me know – how shall I forget.

Life is . . . a Review

The grass you pass has cut so few
Of all that came and never knew

A flower reveals itself in spring
Yet the bulb is just an ugly thing

Your life alone where I had set
There'd be to me withheld regret.
Of how I lived, and not been through
Life is a review to you

You cast your eyes, to what I've seen
You find today – tomorrow's dream
Only hearts can be in love
Only one may be thought of
And though our time may not break through
Life is a review to you

9

Once upon a past, I lived upon a time
Of destined dreams of someone, I no longer call mine
How was I in love, if now I say I'm not
Should you be the future – or is this what I sought?
I only took each passing day to mean there'd be one more
And dreamed about tomorrow, believing I was sure
But time has proved a coward, I can't live up to you
I know not of tomorrow – the calling was undue
Maybe you are sorry, I say I never lied
I fell for you intensely, my feelings cannot hide
Maybe I'm a fool – for displaying my love
But for most of this year, you're all that I thought of
I haven't changed my mind, but I still come to say
If I can't have tomorrow – you don't deserve today.

Could That Be The Rain

Could that be the rain…listen hear it fall,
Although it's clear and cloudy, it's much to close too call

You'd have to be out in it, to sense what you regret
Though it may not be raining, you'd still be getting wet

It could be off the trees, at the mercy of the winds
Like the sudden tears of happiness, as they wait to be condemned

It could from the sky, a rain intent and true
To be part of your morning, your night and afternoon

Just how can you be sure, that it's really really rain
You may have been deceived, misguided and misnamed

The only way to tell, is to stay out of the woods
Wait until the wind stops, and imagine if you could

A gentle fleet of raindrops, insisting they exist,
You'll be soaking wet, if this thing persists.

Equilibrium

Equilibrium is my friend,
But I tend to get bored with him
I'll be on this ride
All eaten up inside
And I'll want it to stop
Then there's another drop
I'll long for the day
When I can just stay
Safe and sound
My feet on the ground
Forever at rest
Until and unless
I get bored ya know
And I have to go

Smile Casting

Far into this rainy night, I cast a smile your way
I'm lost upon the subtlety of what you didn't say

Gathered in a raindrop, somewhat like a tear
I hope to find a yesterday within the coming year

I live to fall upon your heart, you live to see I do
I dream to have the courage, to one day dream of you

I believe in yesterday, for there I've lived and died
I cannot find tomorrow, for there you don't reside

If my wisdom grew a heart, perhaps I'd learn and know
There is honor in the sacrifice, to simply let it go

But time will bring the seasons, to listen and pretend
I may not know the reasons, for the things I will condemn

At least I had the courage to offer you a smile
Please know that will be with me, for just a little while

Faces Blue

Faces blue of the light to show
One I'd seemed to come to know
To be allowed to be there more
Than those who held her fate in store
For me to be along her way
Would give me thoughts not to display
So words would come before my touch
Yet words to me would be enough
Still time revealed a certain end
To see me leave to be a friend
For distance far would take its toll
Yet this is not why we unfold
'Twas change of life and change of way
No kiss goodbye?, no words to say

She Gets It From Us

So much of what she does
We think it is because
Of something she has seen
On a computer or TV screen
And some of that is true
But most is from me and you
She picks up on our way
And the things we say
She wants to be her mom
And draws her cuteness from
Being with all of us
Like the wheels on the bus
We who hang around
Are the reason she astounds

This Worldly Time

Once upon this worldly time, this one was strange to me
Those who took us on would find that we be enemies
This long and lonely time we had was undisputed war
Yet this will seldom leave me sad for this time be no more
Our time began, or so I thought though at least it seemed
But in the past I was still caught to live endless redeem
Though history plagued not my soul my heart appeared relieved
So unto all I shall be cold yet all shall be deceived
See dawn to dusk would ever last and ever would it seem
You would be a part of past I've sought to ever dream
Now left to me I would decide not who I would be-friend
Just how long I would abide the thoughts the past would end
So here I stand for you I'll be forever standing near
Just let this all be history, the past of yester year

Shadows of My Emptiness

Days for some will fall between
Of what's to come, of what's been seen
Of what's been hard and what's been told
This dream deferred will now unfold

A light to pass might cast its way
The darkness shadows things I say
The morning glow receives the dawn
My endless plight will linger on

The time to pass falls short of the dream
The time to last ain't what it seems
Yet if the laughter brings a tear
Cast the time in spite of fear
And reach ahead, - a dream exists
In the shadows of my emptiness

Senior Sonnet
1977

Will you remember this blade of grass
Will you recall the years to pass
Or will you cut this blade of green
And live to hate the years between
For now's the time to bring the thought
Of what's been learned and what's been taught
The time to come may not hold true
To all of what is told of you
For in your prime your time did sing
Of lust and love and wishful things
For all you speak and shall once say
I live tomorrow for yesterday
And in your life it will be known
A rolling past gathers no stone

Wanted

I wanted you to know
I wanted many things
I know will never be
I wanted to explain
I wanted one more chance
I wanted just to hold you
I wanted one more dance
I wanted you to ask me
I wanted to pretend
I wanted to go back
I want to want again
I wanted you to know
I wanted to let go

The Radio
Circa '75

Listening to the radio, P-G-C in stereo
Play'n hits I don't know, wait'n for some Chicago
Ever try M-O-D, or K-Y-S on 93
All the songs are the same to me, Elton John in Harmony
Then click at 6 to 95, Wolfman Jack from New York live
Soft as soul to take a dive, clear-a-sil ain't no jive
Then comes Murph on 1310, play'n tunes from way back when
Story lady read'n sin, wait'n for the world to end.
Then there's stuff like C-F-L, late at night it comes in well
Sometimes you can't even tell, that's when you've been put through hell.
'Course there's D-C – 1 – 0 – 1, freaks and Jon love this one,
As for me I have no fun, I live in love away from none
That is all that I shall say, It's what I heard upon this day
Mama Queen will have to stay, but does it matter anyway

Last Day of Hope

Could this be the last day of hope
The last sunrise I have to cope
With thinking that I have more time
Only the past and today is mine
Not everyone can see the end
As if it's coming and contend
With smiling faces who don't know
You're on the last part of your road
So much promise, and then somehow
My body's working against me now
But it's just a thing we all face
The day we have to leave this place
And tomorrows are for everyone else
But I'll take this day for myself

Tell Me That You Know

I am walking away, and I'm not looking back
This train just goes one way, and now it's on the tracks
But I can't get by your kiss, it stops me at the door
I know it's time to go, then I come back for more
It takes away my breath, and swallows up my words
And the will to speak the truth, as if it would be heard
All I can do is hold you, and want to let you go
There's no way to explain, just tell me that you know
I cannot say goodbye, and I may not speak at all
This may not be over, but I'm not prepared to fall
I've decided not to chase you, as if you could be caught
As if I held the future, and for the moment I do not
But leave the door un-locked, just in case – you know,
I find that I am lonely, and need a place to go

Standing in the Window

I'm standing in the window, I believe the screen is gone.
The sash is dark is and hazy, in the light of early dawn.

This used to be a door, a place of hinge and key –
A passage used so often, left 'tween you and me.

I'm standing in the window, I'm reaching for the door
I'm calling out your name – You call for me no more

Was this a door, I once passed thru, I see no hinge or key
Just pathway plagued by emptiness, left 'tween you and me

A door stood here as I stood there, cast upon the wind
Time remains for what sustains, the beginning and the end

I fall forth to grasp the knob, and find a sash held tight
Yesterday I found my way, today I found the night

I turn away in solitude, to glance at my despair
I'm left without a dream to dream, and without a care to care

Terror Is Part Of The Deal

Who are we, and how do we act
In spite of the truth, the lies and the facts
How often do we just say because
I can't do what someone else does
Or no one has done this – so far
Then no one can see what you truly are
How you could be if you didn't care
That someone judged and you can't bare
To be the candle with the twisted wick
To be the flame that's authentic
To not succumb to the fear
That cause a life to be in-sincere
And act in spite of how you feel
And know that terror is part of the deal.

One Must Take

One must take
What one does give
Before they wake
To why they live
Before they die
They may perceive
The reasons why
I believe
The dark prevails
Everywhere
As I am hailed
In my despair
To leave the past
To those who care

Together

I tend to call your name, though it seems I'm never home
And there's always too much time that we are both alone
You always have a smile, no matter what I do
I'll always come back home, cause always there is you
We must change with the seasons, and how we spend our time
Or else these flowers we have planted will wither up and die
Your smile is in my heart, your touch is but a dream
Your forever's and ever's are my tomorrows it seems
The sunlight cast a spark in the darkness of your face
The moon has left its mark and you carry it with grace
I reach beyond tomorrow, claiming your despair
I have heard the silence inside what you declare
Our life has not been boring, as the lines on our face will show.
Whatever lays before us, together we shall go

There are - - Times

There are times when you are quiet, when I know you want to scream,
And the times you hold it in, last forever it seems

There is a comfort in the silence, and the darkness that you own,
You trust what you can't see, as you fear all you have known

If words could carry sunlight, there's a chance they might reveal,
The shadows in the whispers, and the lies of how you feel

You may stumble in the darkness, of what you feel inside
Best to just keep this quiet, you can say you never tried

For in the power of the moment, I'm helpless in your eyes,
The clouds may block the sun, but they cannot block the sky

From bringing on the storms, that's your cue to go,
The thunder marks your exit, but there's still no way to know

If it's ever gonna rain, and wash this all away
Maybe it won't matter, if there's nothing left to say.

Unforgettable

Yeah, I'm still here, even though you're gone,
There's nowhere else to go, there is no other song

You're everywhere I go, in everything I do,
You have become my shades, you color all I view

I know I have tried to think about you less,
Sometimes I go all day, resisting to obsess

You're not just in my head, you're not just in my heart,
You're in my old brown sweater and every verse I start

There is no place to put you, to keep you locked away,
And if I had you here now I don't know what I'd say

I don't have the answers, I don't know the words,
I don't know how we got here, at 4th and absurd

I've lost all perspective, I don't know who to blame,
I know I can't forget you, and I'll never be the same.

Till You Leave

Long as I've
Been alive,
no one chose to stay
Yet I see more
Of what's in store,
Because you
came this way
You seem to care
As I held you there,
my eyes would not deceive
Just how I feel
I love you still,
And I will, love you
till you leave

I'll Never Understand

Within the heart's companion, the tensions run so deep,
The mind can't overcome the memories we keep
The subtle and the sudden, seem to all be wrong
It soon gives way to fever, and the sickness makes us strong
In the morning it will be raining, as the evening begs the clouds
I welcome all the darkness to come in and sit down
For I may hold a light, to make this look okay
Yet that won't change the night, or hasten on the day
Perhaps you're in the shadow, but why would you be coy,
While you inflict your sorrow, or the sanctity of joy
Why release emotions, in the posture that you hate
Why allow the mood to just precipitate
I may not know the morning, in the darkness we have shared
I will never understand, the way you show you cared

Tomorrow

Tomorrow I'll knock on the door,
Tomorrow I'll say something more
Tomorrow I'll do nothing wrong
Tomorrow I'll sing a different song
Tonight please try to understand
Tonight I've done all that I can
Tonight I don't know what to say
Tonight is not going my way
Tonight you came into view
Tonight I tried to make a move
Tomorrow I want you to see
Tomorrow there's something about me
Today when I look into your eyes
Tomorrow I know I will be alive

Revealing Sonnet

Have your say, if you must
If you think you're on the cusp
Of understanding what I mean
Why the words are in between
What you want and think belongs
In place of words you think are wrong
And could it be that I meant this
Or could it be that you just
Do not know me or my pain
Or the way that I explain
How I feel and how I've shown
In verse and tense and undertone
Something special you can't see
As I reveal a part of me.

Newly Fallen Snow

Upon the seams of purity, of the newly fallen snow
The wind will pass with silence, forsaken by the glow
What besets the white canvas that falls in between
A lonely rabbit lingers on – unraveling the scene
Although the rabbit treads the snow, the footprints can't be seen
The weather comes before the time can pass or intervene
For what may be the treason, of this one's dissent
Abolishing the snow – as if it has consent
Yet this is part of living, as destiny's reviewed
Fate cannot be pleasant if the calling was undue
So no one now can follow – or pass upon this road
For none can share the journey – or lighten up the load
But in your only passing – you do not pass alone
We will have no tomorrow – just the yesterday's we've known

There Were Two

If there were two, to come above,
All your thoughts of perished love
And one of them is love you see
The other once could always be

Would it be sane to sing this song
To spend your nights where you belong,
Or might one leave to under-go
The likes of one you'd like to know

The words of this are in the dream
That calls each night to make it seem
That if you give your heart and soul
There is none left to be controlled
So one must leave to cast away
The heart you've held until this day

The Magic

There are days when the magic hides
And the moment's moment is left inside
And the art recedes into the bay
Carrying the sand and the words that may
Slide down my pen and fall on the page
Igniting emotions that are meant to assuage
The anger pounding along with my heart
For the waste of the will and my part
In losing the vision I wanted to see
And letting the day get the best of me
By stealing the powers I use to share
To dissect and describe the reasons I care
Without a verse and without a rhyme
I will call on the magic another time.

I Can't Explain

I can't explain this need in me
I feel compelled – repeatedly
To gather thoughts that come around
In a certain way with a certain sound.
This isn't normal, but I don't care
I am not alone but it's pretty rare
Not like a journal of different things
It's more like a story that you could sing
Kind of like something I'm searching for
Like a moment, or a memory or a metaphor
So why do these words arrive in this way
Who understands what I'm trying to say
I know these words are meant to be found
And all I can do is write them down.

Writing

This is where I live, and this is how I breathe,
This is who I am, the one no one can see

I am not ashamed, that's not why I hide
All the words I write, 'bout the way I feel inside

I'm not sure it matters, if it isn't very good,
Or if I can explain, or even if I would,

Let you in the door, and lead you down the stairs,
To the cellar I preserve, for all the things I care

I don't want you to judge, I don't want you to know,
How sensitive I am, and how it comes and goes

I'll seek my own counsel, when I take pen in hand,
I scribble raw emotions, and try to understand,

The maybes in the moments, and what comes in between
The poetry and the prose, that never will be seen.

Not a Song

Maybe it's not a song, just because it rhymes,
Because it has a rhythm, and plays in four-four time

Maybe it's just a poem, just bits of verse and words
To think that I could write a song would be absurd

Perhaps if I could sing it or maybe hum along
You could find a melody, and see where I went wrong

Cause if it's just a poem, they will never understand
What I'm trying to say, or even if I can

Translate my emotion, into something people hear
Beyond a greeting card for someone I hold dear

Then all my thoughts are lost, and will never come again
They might as well have stayed inside of my pen

Cause if it's not a song, that someone wants to share
I wonder why I try, when no one else will care

*"Anything I can sing, I call a song.
Anything I can't sing, I call a poem."*

Bob Dylan, from the liner notes of
"The Freewheelin' Bob Dylan - 1963"

Songs Are About Something

Songs are about something…
Something that has to be said
Something you can't understand
And you can't get it out of your head
So you've got to work it through
You've got to write it down
And sing it from your soul
No matter how it sounds.

It could be a pretty face
Or when something's about to start
Like when she smiles your way
Or you are about to part
The song will tell the story
And no two are the same
Like women, wine and whisky
These things can't be explained
Without the special sounds
Like the strumming of the chords
A drum beat keeping time
And some magic rhyming words

Songs Are About Something

(Continued)

One day I'll write a song
To reach the common man
    One day I'll write a verse
They think they understand
    It will touch them all
In places they remember
    And I will never tell them
The song is about her....

Now you can sing along
Just the hook or every line
    And feel it in your bones
It makes everything just fine
    But you may never know
There's something you can't see
    In the song you've been singing
And why it came to be
    A melody with a mood
That might be easy to play
    But the song is about something
That someone had to say

One day I'll write a song
To reach the common man
    One day I'll write a verse
They think they understand
    It will touch them all
In places they remember
    And I will never tell them
The song is about her....

It's Been A While

I know it's been a while, but I am here today
You look really good, but you always looked that way
    I'm sorry I've been busy, chas'n dreams of what could be
Now I don't know what to do, I kind of got lost you see
    I've had a little trouble, and I've seen some things
I didn't know how to start, or what kind of flowers to bring
    But I knew I had to get here, now I don't know what to say
I know it's been a while, but now, everything's okay
I always liked this place, and I often thought of you
Lying in that bed is my million dollar view

    Damn my restless soul, and what I thought I lacked
I knew I had to go, and I knew I had to come back
    I have to say I've grown, as I made my course correction
As I rambled down the roads, and I rendered my reflection
    I'd like to say I'll stay, but promises aren't my style
God it's great to see you, ya know, it's been a while

It's Been A While

(Continued)

I should have come before, but something always came up
You're like a jelly doughnut, and coffee in my cup
I forgot how you taste, and what you're like to touch
And what it's like to kiss you, and hold you and such
And how you kept the faith, and forgave the things I've done
And try to understand, what you think I have become
But now I feel at home, and I thought this would be strange
I know it's been a while, and I'm not the only thing that's changed.

What Kind of Moon

What kind of moon climbs the sky
With the dawning of the night
Slipping silent into view
Humbled by the light.
Shades of grapefruit in the gray
Cast among the clouds –
A beacon for the twinkling star,
The cue ball draws a crowd.

Every night I seek the moon,
And the story must be told,
It's the mirror of my sunshine
And the answer for my soul,
As if I could hold it in my hand,
Like a milk dipped Oreo,
Or lather in the limelight,
Like Joe versus the Volcano.

I tip my hat to the moon
As it conquers another day
What kind of moon climbs the sky
And portends to light my way....

Each night I try to find it,
As I know you're looking too,
I don't know what to call it,
I am hoping maybe you do.
At times it tries to hide,
Or is caught in the trees I fear
Then it pops up like a ping pong ball
That just landed in my beer

What Kind of Moon

(Continued)

I've seen the moon go blue,
In the shape of a frying pan
    It makes me want to travel
And look for Moonlight Graham
    Sometimes it's like the bobber
On the end of a fishing pole
    And then some nights I swear
The moon had done got stole

I tip my hat to the moon
As it conquers another day
    What kind of moon climbs the sky
And portends to light my way....

We share the moon every night
It's the one thing we both can see
    I hope you catch the crescent
And have a moment to think about me
    Cause when the sun goes down
It's just me and you and the moon
    Know that you are not alone
And that I will be there soon

I tip my hat to the moon
As it conquers another day
    What kind of moon climbs the sky
And portends to light my way....

I Won't Think of You

These things are done in person, one on one, face to face
I wanted neutral territory; I wound up at her place
     It started with a hug, and the warmth began to grow
She kept holding tight, 'til she realized I'd already let go
     I couldn't look her in the eye, or let her see my pain
Or say that I was leaving, and would never come back again
     I didn't have to tell her I was there to say goodbye
We both knew it was over, and we both believed that lie

She clung to me like a life raft, I hung onto her cause I cared
And when the storm was over, she was no longer scared
     But she liked being with me better than being alone
And she'll decide that she loves me, the second I am gone

We danced around the issue; she shuffled me toward her bed
Always her best move, as she ignored everything I said
     This wasn't going to work, and I could not explain why
And I didn't want to fight, and I no longer wanted to try
     To keep something going that was bound to fall apart
And at least one of us would end up with a broken heart
     Just know that I once loved you, and that will have to do,
And now and then I'll have a day, when I won't think of you

I Won't Think of You

(Continued)

She clung to me like a life raft, I hung onto her cause I cared

And when the storm was over, she was no longer scared

But she liked being with me better than being alone

And she'll decide that she loves me, the second I am gone

Losing

I pulled into the driveway and walked her to the door
Then she said goodbye, like she never had before
I can't get that look she gave me erased from my head
And I can't stop thinking: Was there something I could have said?

They just called my number, it's a club with double ham,
I'll have to go without the beer, in spite of what I am.
Just a quarter's worth of coffee, when dreams are 35,
I'm a dollar short of caring, when it costs just to survive.

It was cold enough to snow, in the light of pending rain,
I was old enough to know I was not too old for pain.
I find myself insisting on dreams of yester-year,
The pickles and the toothpicks make it classy here

I'll try to think tomorrow, and not the day before.
I'll call the past the sorrow, I'm lost in the either – or.
I'll call the coffee love, and cast it from my soul –
Surrounded by the empty night I have lost all control

How was I to know just how much I lost
Just how many dreams just casually got tossed
I can't hear her voice, I can only see her face
I'm never coming back to that goddamn place

Losing

(Continued)

How empty is the void we call remember when
How hidden are the treasures of fortunes on the wind
Has time brought forth the story, the past has yearned to tell
Is it lost upon the silence of yonder clanging bells?

Pain can be a profit and deliver what is feared
And cast to its disciples what must be revered
It couldn't work this time, it isn't what it seems
In the morning we would wake up and find it's just a dream

It's something like a rainbow without the pot of gold
The vision is the treasure, be happy with what you hold
There are no magic endings, to the stories I can tell
So let's just leave the wishes at the bottom of the well

And they can fill the void, like the seasons and the rain
For the moments we have had, will never come again
But I will not forget you, or the kindness you have shown
If I had another beer, my heart could be atoned
And I could take the steps and let my life unfold
Surrounded by the empty night I'll finally take control

How was I to know just how much I lost
Just how many dreams just casually got tossed
I can't hear her voice, I can only see her face
I ain't never going back to that goddamn place

Another Dream

Do you have another dream? Do you have another thought?
From here at least it seems, your life is easily brought
You give up every day, and make a bargain for your time
Have you ever thought of saying, I'm stepping out of line
You can take my turn, this ain't what it seems
I think it's time I learned, to have another dream

Every morning's like a treadmill, going nowhere in a hurry
And every night's the same - the stress, the bills – the worry
And my heart is beating heavy, when I crawl into my bed
And I pray to God to let me, just try and clear my head
And remember that we used to have time for family and fishing
We smiled when the sun rose, and did something more than wishing

Some other dreams may come between all your obligations
There was a day when you would say without hesitation
I have thoughts of my own, capabilities I have not shown
To any one – any where, because my heart cannot bear
To lose the faith and what it means
To lose the chance to have another dream

Another Dream
(Continued)

Some may follow their fathers, and some will go off to war

For some the pills and the bottle will pretend to offer more

I don't mean to judge, I am no better than you

I haven't learned that much, from the journey I've been through

But now I seem addicted to this day to day grind

With my heart and soul conflicted as I prostitute the time

That I have left to show, what my life could mean

Is it too late for me, to have another dream?

Some other dream may come between all your obligations

There was a day when you would say without hesitation

I have thoughts of my own, capabilities I have not shown

To any one – any where, because my heart cannot bear

To lose the faith and what it means

To lose the chance to have another dream

When You Crawl in Bed With Me

    I pray for another sunrise
From my heart on bended knee
    With the faith that I can stand
And I'll have somewhere to be
    I pray that I can walk
Until the sun goes behind the trees
    Because the best part of my day
Is when you crawl in bed with me

    When you crawl in bed with me
And you know I've had a day
    We don't have to talk about it
There's nothing left to say
    I love you is not spoken
We know that we're okay
    We share a goodnight kiss
And a peaceful place to lay

When You Crawl in Bed With Me
(Continued)

I didn't know the power
Of slipping on that ring
  To stand and say I do
Was such a simple thing
  This year has not been kind
There were things we couldn't see
  Still I held onto you
While you held onto me
  And we made it through the day
Like Piglet and Winnie the Pooh
  Until the covers get pulled back
And I climb into bed with you

  I might be yesterday's news
If tomorrow never came
  My novel reads like a novelty
For what I can't explain
  I don't know what to do
And I don't know what to say
  I just take another breath
And obsess and then decay
  I'll get hold of my rudder
And keep the horizon in view
  I find the purpose of my life
When I crawl in bed with you

Time

I always seem so busy, always on the move
Always on the run, with a list of things to do
I just want to get ahead, to a place just in my mind
No matter what I do, I end up using time.
Time was on my side, when I was just a kid
I had all I needed, for everything I did
But now it's running out, and I'm still running around
It's time for me to notice that my watch is winding down

I used to have a vision, and then I had a plan
I had the kind of obsession people don't understand
And I'm still on that road, I'm just a little behind
But now I'm starting to wonder if I'm running out of time

I can get up before dawn, before the seeds are sewn
Before the boss is in, to claim some for my own
But it never lasts too long, these moments to myself
Soon I find I'm doing something for someone else
I don't think I'm noble, or that I'm on some quest,
I know what I want to do before I'm laid to rest
This is what I love, to create what's in my mind.
But that's not how I live – and I'm running out of time.

I used to have a vision, and then I had a plan
I had the kind of obsession people don't understand
And I'm still on that road, I'm just a little behind
But now I'm starting to wonder if I'm running out of time

Time

(Continued)

I could have lived each day, like it was my last
For a guy with no future, at least I have a past
    Still every day I wake up with a new dream to build
I may only place a few stones - but still
    I can see it form, and come into this world
Something to be shared, between me and my girl
    And I have to see it happen, it's more than a goal
I've got one more dream to dream, before time takes its toll.

*   I used to have a vision, and then I had a plan*
I had the kind of obsession people don't understand
*   And I'm still on that road, I'm just a little behind*
But now I'm starting to wonder if I'm running out of time

I Think I Got Today

So far I'm keeping it together, in focus with the day
I'm locked into this moment, keeping my fears at bay
    It's a good one too, I was here for the rising sun
I have to notice everything – I may not get another one

    I can think of yesterday, and that might make me smile
And lord knows we're only here for just a little while
    I have so much to celebrate, that should make it okay
I'm not ready for tomorrow, but I think I got today.

    Today I can deal, I am already here
I can do what I have to do, and still act sincere
    I can handle what's in front of me, looking in my eyes
I don't have to contemplate, commit or rationalize
    What may happen in the future, and what she might say
I've got no plans for tomorrow, but I think I got today.

    Today has to be enough, there are things that have to be said
As the sun completes its journey, my heart and soul are fed
    I may not have the time, to accomplish everything
But I have come to know, there's a song that I must sing
    While sailors go to see, and farmers cut their hay
I may have no horizons, but at least I've got today

I Think I Got Today
(Continued)

I don't fear tomorrow, I'm not afraid to see

All the consequences coming due for me

I don't look over my shoulder – I'm not on the run

I've left no wrath for an epitaph, if in fact I am done

And if tomorrow finds me, not inside a grave

I will begin again, to live my life that day

So far I'm keeping it together, in focus with the day

I'm locked into this moment, keeping my fears at bay

It's a good one too, I was here for the rising sun

I have to notice everything – I may not get another one

I Give Up

I remember that first look
I remember the way I felt
     The tractor beam in eyes of green
And a smile where dreams are held.

     I didn't know much about her
But I didn't have much to lose
     Her body had its own language
And she didn't like to wear shoes.

*   I lost the power to be cool*
I forgot the rules of the game
*   I could only render my surrender*
I give up – what's your name?

     I had to hear her speak
And watch her toss her hair
     I didn't know why she was a little bit shy
But I wasn't moving from there

     I had found my home
Right there beside of her
     I was smitten – maybe cupid bitten
And I still haven't found the cure

I Give Up
(Continued)

She had to have my children
I would never be the same
My life was saved the night I got brave
And said, "I give up – what's your name?"

I could not look away
I could not control myself
I wanted to know her name
And then I get to everything else.

I'd get to favorite color
And if she liked this song
Then all the kissing I'd been missing
Would eventually come along.

I lost the power to be cool
I forgot the rules of the game
I could only render my surrender
I give up – what's your name

Outlive You All

You can do what you want, you can sit on your couch and drink
You can laugh at what I do, I don't care what you think
I'm gonna climb that mountain, I'm going to make that call
And even if I die, I'm gonna outlive you all

I was born under a half-baked moon, a twinkle from a star
And raised by loving folks, who always raised the bar
And challenged me to be whatever I thought I could
Turns out it was up to me, whether or not I would

I'll write my own life story - I'll finally tell it all
I'll convene from scene to scene, to pen my rise and fall.
I've touched so many people, and they've touched my heart a bit
They come and go and never know, exactly where they fit,
I'll try to find a way, for you to comprehend,
I'd write it now, if I knew how, the storyline would end
I'm not saying I won't lose, but I'll never admit defeat
That day when my number's up and they hand me that receipt
I'll know I lived and loved more than anyone I ever knew
So unless you get off your ass, I'm going to outlive you

You can do what you want, you can sit on your couch and drink
You can laugh at what I do, I don't care what you think
I'm gonna climb that mountain, I'm going to make that call
And even if I die, I'm gonna outlive you all

Outlive You All

(Continued)

I don't have much talent, and I don't have the skills
But I went after it all and I found I had the will
To go with all my heart after every single dream
Even if I failed, and even while it seems
There is no earthly chance I ever would achieve
I had the guts to try and faith enough to believe
I was here for a purpose, that you can't find at the Mall
My destiny is to find it, as I outlive you all

You can do what you want, you can sit on your couch and drink
You can laugh at what I do, I don't care what you think
I'm gonna climb that mountain, I'm going to make that call
And even if I die, I'm gonna outlive you all

Used to Be

Maybe you remember me, from my brief brush with glory
I don't have much to show for that, now it's just a story
I thought that was the moment when I would break out
But what followed was too much whiskey, desperation and doubt

I used to be somebody – somewhere back in the day
I used to have a vision, and you'd see things my way.
I used to wake up happy, and everything was fun
I used to have a plan, and the will to get things done.

I don't know what happened; I don't know when I got scared
I don't know when I gave up, or the last time somebody cared
I let fear get a grip on the thoughts back in my head
And I forgot you have to forget, what everyone else has said.

I used to stand up straight and walk without the pain,
I used to make an entrance and people knew my name.
I used to really mean it when I said I'd be there,
I used to have more patience, I used to really care.

I don't want your pity or that dollar in your hand
I don't need your respect, you don't have to understand
That what I am today is not what I used to be
And you will sing this song….eventually

Used to Be
(Continued)

I used to make a difference, back when I had respect,

I used to hide it well, sarcasm and contempt.

I used to solve the problems, that people brought to me

I used to have solutions, that others could not see.

I used to have a dream, that it would be okay,

I used to have the faith, that I had something to say

Maybe you remember me, from my brief brush with glory

I don't have much to show for that, now it's just a story

I thought that was the moment when I would break out

But what followed was too much whiskey, desperation and doubt

Come With Me

    I see you've been watching
And I've been watching you
        Wondering what you're like
And what you are up to
        If I just walked right over
As smooth as I could be
        If I could make you smile
Would you come with me

        I don't know where we're going
And I don't know what we'll do
        But I feel like I can do anything
If I can be with you
        You make it to my truck
And you take off your shoes
        Open the door for me
At that moment I knew
        I had found a gal
That suits me to a Tee
        And the world was mine
Cause you decided to come with me

Come With Me
(Continued)

I've always felt left out
When they called the couples dance
I've had a girl before
But I've never had romance
I never felt the tickle
Deep down in my belly
And when I try to stand
My knees both turn to jelly
When I saw you tonight
My whole life made sense
And when you came with me
I gave up my defense

I opened up my heart
You opened up my mind
I forgot where I was
And I lost all track of time
I entered a new realm
Where dreams become a plan
Where impossible things
I began to understand
Like I never had before
A life I couldn't see
Until you took my hand
And decided to come with me

First Christmas Without You

I don't know how to do this
I didn't think it would be this hard
 Should have left that box in the basement
And that tree, out in the front yard
 They say go through the motions
But they don't know my life
 They say it will get better
But they didn't know my wife
 And how everything around me
Reminds me to remember
 There'll be no presents for me
It's my first Christmas without her

 I've tried to be merry
And I've tried to be strong
 White Christmas comes on the radio
And I try to sing along
 I try to smile at Santa
As he's ringing that damn bell
 But I'm feeling more like Rudolf
Lost in misfit toy hell
 I try to let the season
Not be the reason for my pain
 It's my first Christmas without her
And it looks like it's gonna rain

First Christmas Without You
(Continued)

I even went to Church

Sang the hymn and said a prayer

I understand I'm not alone

But I see her everywhere

In the faces of my children

And the flannel shirts she got me

Every snowman Christmas ornament

And every Cinnamon Dolce Latte

I can't hear one more jingle bell

Keep your frankincense sense and myrrh

I'm holding onto scotch and dreams

For my first Christmas without her

Good Time

If you're looking my way, you'll have to look again
I may not look interested, or I may just pretend
       To be out of your league, or at least in another class
One thing you can tell, is I'm a man with a past
       I've been around the bend, and I'm from out of town
I'm not here for the coffee, and I won't be hanging around
       So don't be acting coy, when you're giving me the eye
If you're looking for a good time, you're gonna be surprised

I want to be intrigued, and I want you to be amazed
If you're looking for a good time, with me, the bar's been raised
       I'm not trying to convince you, with anything I've said
But you seem like a good reason for me to turn my head
       And what that means to me, is a candle has been lit
So you wanna fan the flames and give this town a fit?

I'm gonna try your patience, I'm gonna make you think
I'm not gonna try and impress you with how much I can drink
       I won't try to make you laugh, but I'd like to see you smile
We won't be playing show and tell, at least for a little while
       I'd like to get to know you, before we lose control
And the blue jeans hit the floor, and you show me that mole

Good Time
(Continued)

I want to be intrigued, and I want you to be amazed
If you're looking for a good time, with me, the bar's been raised
I'm not trying to convince you, with anything I've said
But you seem like a good reason for me to turn my head
And what that means to me, is a candle has been lit
So you wanna fan the flames and give this town a fit?

I've got no time for ordinary, or something merely good
With me you'll do something you never thought you would
We won't spend lots of money, it's kind of hard to explain
We may just have a beer, or we may drink champagne
We might go to a movie, or we might talk to the moon
When you're steppin' out with me, you will not be home soon
So if you're looking for a good time, try that guy over there
But if you're looking for something else, let's get out of here

I want to be intrigued, and I want you to be amazed
If you're looking for a good time, with me, the bar's been raised
I'm not trying to convince you, with anything I've said
But you seem like a good reason for me to turn my head
And what that means to me, is a candle has been lit
So you wanna fan the flames and give this town a fit

I Thought You Liked Me

I thought maybe you liked me
I thought we were having fun
About the time I thought we were fine
Was about when you were done

You always wanted to go out
You liked to really romp and play
The way you act was true in fact
In spite of the things you'd say

The way you moved your body
Let me misread your mind
You wanted it all as we began to fall
In love for the very first time

You see I got confused
This wasn't what I thought
Now I've learned - I'll just return
That diamond ring I bought
I won't say that I'm sorry
That's just not how I feel
How could I ever know forever
Would take so long to heal

I could tell you were holding back
The feelings you never set free
Turns out I was wrong all along
You were just fond of me

I Thought You Liked Me
(Continued)

I get that something happened
And someone hurt you – okay
There's love and lust but you'll never trust
Someone to be there every day

So you let yourself have fun
But your heart's not in the game
While I'm holding on you are long gone
And I will never be the same

I don't think you are broken
I just think it's sad
You missed your chance in this circumstance
For the best thing you ever had

You see I got confused
This wasn't what I thought
Now I've learned - I'll just return
That diamond ring I bought
I won't say that I'm sorry
That's just not how I feel
How could I ever know forever
Would take so long to heal

The Harmonica

So I have this harmonica
That I don't know how to play
    I can blow a couple notes
And sometimes it sounds okay
    It belonged to my granddad
He left this world too soon
    So I guess it's up to me
To come up with my own tune

It's doesn't have to be perfect
It could even be a little wrong
    It could just be something for me
No one else has to sing along
    Then why am I afraid
To come up with my own song

This may take some patience
The kind I don't have at this age
    Much like the faith of a child
To follow the steps on the page
    And know it will take some time
To find out where songs come from
    So I should be content to play
She'll be coming around the mountain....when she comes

It's doesn't have to be perfect
It could even be a little wrong
    It could just be something for me
No one else has to sing along
    Then why am I afraid
To come up with my own song

The Harmonica
(Continued)

I can almost hear the music
When I quiet down my mind
I'd swear that is a melody
With a rhythm of some kind
It has my head a noddin'
And my foot's tappn' on its own
It's time to take a deep breath
Close my eyes and just go

I don't care if you like it
I don't know if it's good
This came from inside of me
Where I didn't know it could
I think I'll play it again
And this time I'll play it loud
So maybe he will hear it
And my Granddad will be proud

I don't think that it's perfect
I probably played it all wrong
Maybe you could play it
And then I could sing along
Then you would have the courage
To come up with your own song

What Are We Waiting For

Maybe we're not ready, maybe you don't think you can
Maybe you've got something to do; have you met a better man?
Maybe you are scared and you think there's something to lose
So what are you waiting for? You know it's just an excuse

I love when your hair falls in your face - you look better somehow
I like the way you wear that dress and the place we are at now
I love holding hands at sunset, and all our memories
I love every wrinkle in your smile, and how you still look at me

I know that you are with me, and you haven't said never
I don't mean to rush things, but we are coming up on forever
There's a purpose in this place, so let's walk through that door
You can't do this alone, so what are we waiting for?

I've put away my special pen for solitary blues
There'll be no more poems and promise, just songs about loving you
I'm tired of looking back at all the things we did
The way that we once were, will be a story for our kids
This is our ever after, until the laughter turns to tears
And every day I'll live to say I'm glad that you're still here

What Are We Waiting For
(Continued)

I know that you are with me, and you have not said never

I don't mean to rush things, but we are coming up on forever

> *There's a purpose in this place, so let's walk through that door*

You can't do this alone, so what are we waiting for?

Work Through

I know I haven't been myself
There is nothing you can do
        And it's not anything you have done
It's just something I have to work through

        I thought it could be a funk
Or a phase that might just pass
        I don't know how deep this goes
Or how long that it will last
        I'm gonna need some time
And probably a break or two
        I promise you I'll get there
It's just something I have to work through

        I can't see past the storm
To a day where it doesn't rain
        When I can feel the sun on my face
And breathe without the pain
        And momentary melancholy
That does not move along
        When every move I make
Something else seems to go wrong
        I used to believe in myself
I always knew what to do
        But faith and hope have left me
It's just something I have to work through

Work Through

(Continued)

I don't think it's depression
I think it's somewhere in between
  Despair and disillusion
But I don't know what that means
  It's one foot in front of the other
There's a new chance every day
  And I don't know where I'm going
And when I get there what I'll say
  But I know that when the sun sets
I'll be coming home to you
  And one of these days I'll tell ya
Just what I had to work through…

Wants and Needs

What did I need this morning,
A little quiet and a view
What did I want this morning
To write a song for you.

I thought I needed an aspirin
I thought I needed to rest,
I said I would die without coffee
But that's something you say in jest

I need to make a list
But for that I need my brain
To disengage from everything
That's been causing me pain.

I've got so many needs
And I want so many things
But all I want to do
Is find a song to sing
One that she can hear
And hope she understands
That hope is all I need
And I hope she takes my hand

I just need to breathe
I don't have to think
I don't have to contemplate
How the water got into the sink

Just splash it on my face
And let it run down my back
And believe the pain in my chest
Is not a heart attack

Ignore the face in the mirror
The guy who looks like a bum
He does not represent
The person I've become

Wants and Needs

(Continued)

I've got so many needs
And I want so many things
But all I want to do
Is find a song to sing
One that she can hear
And hope she understands
That hope is all I need
And I hope she takes my hand

I'm searching for the strength
To do the things I said
To try and keep my promises
And keep you in my bed

You're not just my lover
You're the best I ever met
It's not just another day
It's the only life I'll get

So I gotta make it count
And make sure that you know
I have to spend my life with you
Even when I have to go

I've got so many needs
And I want so many things
But all I want to do
Is find a song to sing
One that she can hear
And hope she understands
That hope is all I need
And I hope she takes my hand

The Kind of Love That Matters

You're not easy to love
And you're not easy to understand
You're not easy to satisfy
But I'm doing the best I can
You're not easy to live with
And you're not easy to please
You're not easy to travel with
And you're not easy to leave
But we have a love that matters
The kind that won't let go
The kind that people talk about
And sometimes it doesn't know
How close that we can be
And how much we're a team
You are not easy to love
But neither am I it seems

The kind of love that matters
When all my underwear is tattered
When the morning bacon splatters
I'll stir the pancake batter
And pour out maybe a cat or-
Winnie the Pooh but only fatter
And even though our family's scattered
We have the kind of love that matters

You're easy to forgive
Although you never forget
You're harder to make laugh
Than anyone I ever met
You're easy on the eyes
And you're easy to be with
You hold my hand in the mall
And you're always ready for a kiss

The Kind of Love That Matters

(Continued)

You're happy to stay in
Instead of going out
You'll explain the movie to me
When I don't know what it's about
You will share the blankets
Except when it's cold
And you'll still do the dance
Even when we are old
I made a good choice
And that's easy to see
But what I don't know
Is why you chose me...

The kind of love that matters
When all my underwear is tattered
When the morning bacon splatters
I'll stir the pancake batter
And pour out maybe a cat or-
Winnie the Pooh but only fatter
And even though our family's scattered
We have the kind of love that matters

It's What We Do

There's what we do and why we do it
And what we don't regret
And what she says and what she means
And what she won't forget

There's what will happen if we get caught
And when we know we're fine
And then there's what we should have done
And what just seems unkind

I think I learned my lesson
That's what she wants me to say
But she ought to know the next time
I'm going to do it anyway

I'm not sure how we got here
But we're not going back
And she knows that I am sorry
But I seem to have a knack
For making something happen
And then making things okay
She thinks that I am growing
But I don't know another way.

I think I learned my lesson
That's what she wants me to say
But she ought to know the next time
I'm going to do it anyway

It's What We Do
(Continued)

I've made plenty of mistakes
And the world has slapped me down
But each time I'm determined
When I get up off the ground
To go at it again
And not to prove I'm right
Just to prove I have the faith
To hope one day I might
Give her what she wants
And make her proud of me
Then finally I'd become
The man she thought I'd be

I think I learned my lesson
That's what she wants me to say
But what I've come to know
Is that she wakes up every day
Knowing what I am
And knowing that's okay
And If she had the chance
She'd do the same thing anyway

You Don't Know The Pain

You don't know the pain, and you don't know the past
You don't know the reason for this scorched earth and wrath
You don't know what happened, you don't understand
I just can't talk to her – the way you think I can

It's hard for me now, even when I remember
Meeting her that day, the last day of December
She was starting over and I was trying my luck
She played me like a rebound when I started something up
She took me for a ride and didn't buy the car
She didn't say goodbye, that's just the way things are
It lasted to the spring, but then it didn't grow
I asked her what was wrong, she said she didn't know

You think I should call her, just to see how she's doing
Like somehow we're still friends, no matter who she's screwing
Like you know what I'm feeling, you think you can tell
You don't know the pain, and just how hard I fell

You Don't Know The Pain
(Continued)

This is sticking with me, it's not going away
I know I will move on, but maybe not today
And maybe not for a while, maybe not for a year
No matter what you say, no matter how much beer
This one took me deep and I slammed against the wall
I can't imagine a day that I won't want to call
You can say what you want, but do not be concerned
I'll keep looking in this whisky glass to find out what I learned
Until there comes a day, when I want to try again
But you don't know the pain from the path where I have been

You think I should call her, just to see how she's doing
Like somehow we're still friends, no matter who she's screwing
Like you know what I'm feeling, you think you can tell
You don't know the pain, and just how hard I fell

I've Got Things To Do

I lie in bed at sunrise
With my old friend pain
I could make the case – this is my resting place
Or I can get up once again

I best not wake my baby
She's got her troubles too
She counts on me, and well – ya see
I've got things to do

I got myself out the house
And the old truck started okay
There's a heavy dew - still holding on too
As I hold on for one more day.

The sun's get'n ahead of me
I wonder why I still care
I roll the window down and head on into town
I'm not ready but I'm getting there.

I'm holding on to a vision
That I dreamed – when I used to
I won't be told that I'm not in control
Because I've got things to do

People try to push me
But I would rather be drawn
I can't keep pace with the rats in the race
Egging me to come on

I've Got Things To Do

(Continued)

What if I don't go
And I don't mean just today
My hat will tip, I cash in my chips
And I just walk away

I know that is an option
The road goes the other way
But today I'll do what I have to do
And say what I have to say

To be more than just a memory
More like once upon a time
With youth in my past my headstone's been cast
But I can chisel in one more line

I might be getting old
But I've still got a point of view
I don't like the sound of being in the ground
'Cause I've got things to do

The Carousel

I'm trapped inside a carousel
And it won't stop going around
I was on a horse and fell
But I did not hit the ground
Then I tried the unicorn
But I could not hold on
I guess I never learned
To live as a vagabond

Around and round I see tomorrow
And the song that will be played
And I know the sorrow
When the joy begins to fade
I thought this would be fun
Now it's something I must own
Cause when the day is done
I don't want to be alone

I always liked the circus
The lights, the games, the rides
They could never hurt us
Or take that feeling inside
That the world was so exciting
Through the eyes of a kid
Carnival barkers make it inviting
With everything they did

The Carousel
(Continued)

Cotton candy and the ring toss
Would keep me there all day
Until the time I got lost
On the carousel to stay
While everyone stood in line
I was taken for a ride
Send me round one more time
I got nowhere else to hide.

I'm trapped inside a carousel
And it won't stop going around
I was on a horse and fell
But I did not hit the ground
Then I tried the unicorn
But I could not hold on
I guess I never learned
To live as a vagabond

Maybe We Should Go

I like the way she moves
It's a little like a dance
        As if she's talking to me
It's like I have a chance
        Her body has a language
I think I understand
        I'd like to make a move
She makes me think I can
        I'm not the only one
Who sees what's going on
        She's putting on a show
And it won't last too long

Maybe one more whiskey
Or maybe one last beer
        That'll be enough tonight
For me to walk out of here
        Cause I can't stop looking at her
And I've got no more money to blow
        And she is nothing but trouble
So maybe we should go

Maybe We Should Go
(Continued)

I gather up my gall
And I move into her space
    I take her in my arms
And she takes in my gaze
    She looks right through my heart
To the damage in my soul
    And sees something to love
And something she can't control
    She finally takes a breath
And says: "I know you
    That crazy in your eyes
You can see it in mine too"
    Maybe that's enough
For a life and love to grow
    My crazy digs your crazy
So maybe we should go

Maybe one more whiskey
Or maybe one last beer
    That'll be enough tonight
For me to walk out of here
    Cause I can't stop looking at her
And I've got no more money to blow
    And she is nothing but trouble
So maybe we should go

The Secret

Did you ever try to do something
They said could not be done
Did you ever have the thought
That you could be someone
Who could have an idea
And develop it into a plan
And do what you said you'd do
Just because you can

There's a secret to everything
You just have to find out what it is
You have to be willing to swing the bat
No matter how many times you miss
No matter what they say
No matter how long it takes
There is a secret to everything
For every dream you make

So you've tried a million times
And you've even started to start
And people always told you
That was the hardest part
But it's farther down the list
It might even be number three
Number two is make the plan
And one is finishing the thing
So don't be all that proud
That you got something going
Just try to remain focused
All the time you're knowing
That you have the faith
And you have a plan
And you know the secret
Only a few will understand

The Secret
(Continued)

So work up all your courage
And pull out all your gumption
        And expect the unexpected
When it doesn't fit your assumption
        And know you're on a path
That's uphill all the way
        And you can stop and rest
But there's one thing you can't say
        That you are giving up
Cause it's just not meant to be
        The only secret that I know
Is that everything is up to me

There's a secret to everything
You just have to find out what it is
        You have to be willing to swing the bat
No matter how many times you miss
        No matter what they say
No matter how long it takes
        There is a secret to everything
For every dream you make

Solitude

So many voices – so much to say
So many conversations to start the day
So many questions – so many plans
So many things I don't understand
I need to think – I need to breathe
I need to contemplate the things I believe
I need a moment to be with my mind
I can't explain it – everything is fine

When I'm on my own, please don't think it's bad
My brain solves the problems I didn't know I had
I gather my thoughts and what I thought I knew
And look forward to the time I spend with you

I don't want the morning – it's coming too soon
I just spent the night with my best friend the moon
I don't want to move on – I don't want to become
Just another soul who gives in to the sun
There's people on busses and people on trains
People on the sidewalks and the roads are insane
I will not cross the bridge – I'll take to the sea
I'll set course for the horizon – that's where I'm gonna be

Solitude

(Continued)

When I'm on my own, please don't think it's bad
My brain solves the problems I didn't know I had
I gather my thoughts and what I thought I knew
And look forward to the time I spend with you

I don't have a posse – I don't have a clan
I'm a bit of a loner – I'm a one man band
I'm not antisocial, and I don't want to be rude
I can only find sanity in my solitude
I hope you have a place, where you can be you
In a manner and method to match your point of view
A place you don't speak about – even to your friends
For fear that your dreams will only be condemned
And that one glowing ember that warms your soul
Will die in the darkness before your vision unfolds

When I'm on my own, please don't think it's bad
My brain solves the problems I didn't know I had
I gather my thoughts and what I thought I knew
And look forward to the time I spend with you

I Want To Be Alright

I want to be alright, just like the way I was
Yet I embrace the passing of time, and the damage it does
I want to live a life, where dreams are still in view
I want to spend my days and my nights with you

I know I'm not alone, but it doesn't feel that way
I'm face to face with fear, with barely the faith for today
I don't want you to worry, I don't want you concerned
I am always with you, I hope by now you've learned
It's you and me kid, and our baby girls
I never needed anything else from my time on this world.

I understand my struggles and yours are not the same,
Each day brings a new challenge as it deals out its dose of pain
We live for little moments in this life for a little while
We access happy thoughts stored in our memory files.
One day it will all be over, no more dreams to list
For a while they will remember, when I used to exist
I want them to smile, I want them to be okay
I want them to understand what I tried to say
And how I tried to live, how you could count on me
A man of words and deeds, is what I tried to be.

I Want To Be Alright

(Continued)

I know I'm not alone, but it doesn't feel that way

I'm face to face with fear, with barely the faith for today

I don't want you to worry, I don't want you concerned

I am always with you, I hope by now you've learned

It's you and me kid, and our baby girls

I never needed anything else from my time on this world.

Let Her Know

I'm drowsy and I'm sleepy – way too tired to dream
If I did fall asleep what would that even mean?
That today is over and therefore it's time
For today to be a memory lost inside my mind
For me to recall and maybe second guess
My holding on to things that I can't confess
If I could have changed – If I had known
I'd have another sleepless night to own
For letting the moment slip away
For not having the guts to stand up and say
I could do more – I think I still can
I'm more than a fool and less than a man
For letting the day pass me right by
For not saying I love you – after the sigh

Welcome to ever after – not the fiction but the facts
There's a story when the story ends, and a story after that
Everything you wanted is now taken for granted
You're covered by the crop you so carefully planted
You're happy in your heart, but it doesn't always show
You're happy that she stayed – so you ought to let her know

Let Her Know
(Continued)

What was I supposed to think – how was I to feel?
I guess I should have known this was part of the deal
    A little good – a little bad and a little unexpected
More than I could hope for, but less than she suspected
    I had a life and a plan and a journey I was on
Before you and I became a thing, before you came along
    I was on a boat about to go to sea
I got clobbered by your eyes, the day you smiled at me
    And the boat stayed at the dock and I kept my feet on land
I put away childish things and I became a man
    You gave me a life and a reason to get out of bed
A kiss every morning, and children who need to be fed
    And what did I give you, but a roof against the rain
Some moments between the mysteries, some passion with the pain

Welcome to ever after – not the fiction but the facts
There's a story when the story ends, and a story after that
    Everything you wanted is now taken for granted
You're covered by the crop you so carefully planted
    You're happy in your heart, but it doesn't always show
You're happy that she stayed – so you ought to let her know

Hold Off The Morning

Morning has broken, but I just can't do it
I'm sitting in my solitude, trying to get through it
    I didn't want today to be already here
It's still last night I say, 'cause this is last night's beer
    The morning can't be near, 'cause I can't explain
How did I get here and why I feel this pain
    So take this coffee and cream, I'm gonna be alright
As long as I can dream this is still last night

You take your morning, and you get out of town
This is your last warning – I don't like the sound
    Of all those little birds and the train coming down the tracks
I haven't found the words that are going to bring her back

    If it's still last night, I don't have to face the day
I don't have to say she's right, when I don't know what to say
    I can crawl back in my mind where anger is in control
I don't have to face the time when my actions are all tolled
    I need to still remember – at least for a little while
When the morning could be tender and I could make her smile
    Long before I stumbled, and before I made her cry
When I used to be humble and I didn't have to lie

Hold Off The Morning
(Continued)

You take your morning, and you get out of town
This is your last warning – I don't like the sound
   Of all those little birds and the train coming down the tracks
I haven't found the words that are going to bring her back

If I had the power to go back into time
I know the exact hour when I committed the crime
   Of letting her walk away like I didn't care
If that happened today I'd get out of my chair
   I would take her by the hand and I would hold her tight
And make her understand that I don't want to fight
   I have nothing to give and far too many regrets
The only way I live is to drink and to forget

You take your morning, and you get out of town
This is your last warning – I don't like the sound
   Of all those little birds and the train coming down the tracks
I haven't found the words that are going to bring her back

Candlelight Calamities

The smiles are easy in the first conversation
The need to connect and escape desperation
    And push your way forward like a dream giving birth
Like the daffodil bulb laying wait in the earth
    Call upon courage and put your faith in gear
Let go of your worries – let go of your fears
    Let go of the moment you wanted to run
Find out what happens – could this be the one

Candlelight flickers are calling my name
Like a moth that came - I am never the same
    When I get burned I will eventually learn
Too close to the flame is a dangerous game

    To allow yourself to be a little more composed
To sense yourself being a little more exposed
    To become vulnerable may get you attention
To desire her comfort may relieve apprehension
    To look in her eyes and see Sunday morning
To wave off the wine from continually pouring
    And stop showing off and start showing her
Inside of yourself – with a little candor

Candlelight Calamities
(Continued)

Candlelight flickers are calling my name
Like a moth that came - I am never the same
When I get burned I will eventually learn
Too close to the flame is a dangerous game

Listen to her – as if you really cared
Let the silences land - you just like being there
Let the moment happen when the conversation wanes
Catch the look in her eyes when the smile drains
You'll see if it matters – what you've been saying
If she's just being nice because you are paying
Or if you got to her and what you should do
When the candle goes out – if she got to you

Candlelight flickers are calling my name
Like a moth that came - I am never the same
When I get burned I will eventually learn
Too close to the flame is a dangerous game

Old Men Faces

I see it in the mornings
I see the old man stare
It's more than a casual look
And more than a cautious glare
It's less a look and more of a leer
Like they don't know how they got here
Like they're in a moment they can't forget
All of the things they still regret

I see myself in old men's faces
Diners and trains with old suitcases
Theyre life in the lines of expressions unknown
As they wait for the date to be chiseled in stone

It's mostly in the mornings, at least it seems
They're clean and sober – just off their dreams
Before they get busy into the day
And the past is a place they can let lay
Along with the pain of the past that comes
With mornings and thoughts of what they could of done

Old Men Faces
(Continued)

I see myself in old men's faces
Diners and trains with old suitcases
Their life in the lines of expressions unknown
As they wait for the date to be chiseled in stone

It's not all sadness and labored sighs
Sometimes there's a grin, or a twinkle in the eyes
A moment with a meaning will come to pass
That will stay with them until their last
Breath on this earth their heart can bare
Then no more mornings and thousand yard stares

I see myself in old men's faces
Diners and trains with old suitcases
Their life in the lines of expressions unknown
As they wait for the date to be chiseled in stone

Girls With Curls

I kinda like your curly hair
And I kind of like that dress
I like the way you look at me
You make me want to confess
Just what I've been thinking
And what I want to do
Spend every waking moment
Gett'n that dress off of you

I must say I'm intrigued
And a little off my game
I thought I'd meet a girl
But she's more like a dame
Who can't seem to sit still
And I can't follow her
She speaks in hyper similes
And non-linear sequiturs

Girls With Curls
(Continued)

Yeah...I'm over my head
But I really don't care
I've already decided
To follow her anywhere
Find out where it goes
Find out if it's real
Find out if it matters
They way she makes me feel
See if there's something under
That crazy kooky shell
How she looks at me tomorrow
And if I can tell
If she is into me
If I fit in her world
Or if something else is going on
Underneath those curls

I guess I'll never know
This ending can't be told
I can't get past those curls
I'm just not that bold
I tapped my foot and when I looked
You'd stopped looking at me.
Now you're not alone and I'm on my own,
There's him and his iced tea
The moment passed and I got cast
Inside these cement shoes
Who thought chance and circumstance
Could be dressed up like you

I Know The Way

Let's pretend I have a vision
To see beyond today
And know the steps we should take
For us to be okay
Pretend there is a trust
And faith in what I say
Pretend that you believe
Pretend I know the way

I'm not saying you should follow
I'm not saying I should lead
I'm not sure where I'm going
But I've decided to proceed
I don't know if it's right
I don't know what it will be
I know I must go forward
And that's enough for me
I'd like you to come with
Not to follow or obey
You would be by my side
And pretend I know the way

Let's pretend I have a vision
To see beyond today
And know the steps we should take
For us to be okay
Pretend there is a trust
And faith in what I say
Pretend that you believe
Pretend I know the way

I Know The Way

(Continued)

We've come a long way now
And we have to keep going
    In spite of where we are
And which way the wind is blowing
    We cannot go back
We both know where we've been
    If we took the other road
We'd wind up here again
    I promised you a journey
You promised me you'd stay
    And you still look at me
Like I know the way

    Let's pretend I have a vision
To see beyond today
    And know the steps we should take
For us to be okay
    Pretend there is a trust
And faith in what I say
    Pretend that you believe
Pretend I know the way

Words On A Page

What's all this about – what does it mean?
Words on a page, something you have seen
Something you felt – something you could
Contrive into rhyme and then be understood
Like it was important or something true
And something insightful that only you
Could piece together in a special way
Like your words are worth someone's take-home pay

Some call it self-discovery - mired in self-doubt
They're the ones who will never know what it's all about
The hours of anguish, desperation and rage
From the people who put down the words on a page

So why do you do it – why write it down?
And care what it means and how it sounds
When no one will listen and no one will read
No one will care how much that you bleed
How far you'll dig into your soul
How much of the misery you try to unfold
And present your pain as an allegory
At best your suffering becomes a very nice story

Words On A Page
(Continued)

Some call it self-discovery - mired in self-doubt
They're the ones who will never know what it's all about
The hours of anguish, desperation and rage
From the people who put down the words on a page

Perhaps there's a day in the days to come
Perhaps your words will be heard by someone
They will smile and laugh and shed a tear
Applaud and appreciate your purpose here
But until that day, and until that time
You are left alone to wrestle with your rhymes
As if you had something better to do
As if something could mean more to you

Some call it self-discovery - mired in self-doubt
They're the ones who will never know what it's all about
The hours of anguish, desperation and rage
From the people who put down the words on a page

And in case you were wondering…

Forever…More

There is more, there's always more
There's more now than there was before
Another book or two or three
You let me know what you want to read
Cause I don't know anymore
Not like I ever knew before
It just keeps coming out
You decide what it's all about
And what it could be
And what it says about me
And why I write all the time
And generally it tends to rhyme
Until they put me in a drawer
Then there will be no more

www.ingramcontent.com/pod-product-compliance
Lightning Source LLC
LaVergne TN
LVHW061223060426
835509LV00012B/1406